CONTENTS

INTRODUCTION

When you're considering college—or some form of education after high school—financial aid almost always comes to mind.

While you have the primary responsibility of paying for college, sometimes those funds just aren't enough and you need to look at other resources. The U.S. Department of Education provides more than $150 billion in federal student aid (grants, work-study, and loans) each year to students seeking a postsecondary education (a degree after high school). About 14 million students currently receive federal student aid with a majority receiving federal student loans. In addition to federal student aid, financial aid is also available from colleges, companies, private scholarship funds, or the state in which you live. So there are resources to help you pay for college, but you have to utilize them!

As you explore your financial aid options, make sure to consider federal student loans. These loans are a possibility for everyone because not all federal student loans are based solely on financial need. If you have any questions or concerns about getting a federal student loan, then make sure to review this publication.

Why should I read this publication?

If you're thinking about getting a federal student loan, are in the process of obtaining one, or already have one, you should read this publication. This booklet will help you understand the federal student loan process and help you make informed financial decisions.

REMEMBER: *Federal student loans are real loans, just like car loans or mortgage loans. You must repay a student loan even if your financial circumstances become difficult. Federal student loans usually can't be written off in bankruptcy. They can't be canceled because you didn't get the education or job you expected, and they can't be canceled because you didn't complete your education (unless you couldn't complete your education because your school closed).*

Glossary
Definitions of financial aid terms used in this publication can be found in the Glossary on page 37.

PREPARE—Understanding Financial Aid and Your Loan Options

Paying for a postsecondary education (college or trade school) is an investment. It requires planning. It takes money. So talk with your family openly and early. If you're in high school, you can also talk to a guidance counselor at your school; they often have helpful information about planning for a postsecondary education. You also can contact a financial aid office at the college you plan to attend or are considering attending.

How much does college cost?

To determine your total college costs, you should get as much detailed information as you can from schools you are interested in. These costs are usually listed in the college's brochure or on its website. Keep in mind that college costs are not just tuition and room and board. Table 1 provides a description of common college costs.

Table 1.
Description of college costs by selected expenditure items

Item	Description
Tuition	The cost of taking a course varies from school to school. To search for tuition costs at different colleges, go to **www.studentaid.ed.gov/myfsa**.
Room and board	The cost of lodging and food varies from school to school. Go to **www.studentaid.ed.gov/myfsa** to search for estimated costs.
Books and school supplies	Books can be expensive. School supplies can include book bags, notebooks, pens, pencils, paper, folders, stapler, desk organizing system (trays, pen holder, etc.), computer paper, etc. According to the College Board, the national average cost for textbooks at four-year public colleges in 2009–10 was $1,122.
Fees	Fees will depend on the school you're attending. This list can be obtained directly from the school. Fees include activity fees, parking decal fees, etc.
Equipment and room materials	Equipment may include a computer, printer, etc. Furnishings or room materials may include such items as reading lamps, microwave, refrigerator, sheets, towels, etc.
Travel and miscellaneous expenses	If you live on campus, you'll probably need to travel during school breaks. Other expenses can include clothing and cell phone use.

What financial resources are there?

You and your family have the responsibility of planning and paying for college. Your financial resources come from

- scholarships,
- prepaid or college savings plans,
- personal savings, and
- money from work (summer, part-time, etc.).

If you still need additional money, turn to

- the federal government, and
- institutional and state aid.

What is the federal government's role in financial aid?

The federal government is the main provider of financial aid for college. Every year, students and parents receive more than $150 billion in federal student aid. With all these funds available, applying for aid from the federal government is a good option. Federal student aid from the federal government includes:

- **grants**—free money that doesn't have to be repaid, except in some cases when you withdraw from school;
- **work-study**—money you earn to pay for your education;
- **loans**—money you borrow for school, which you must repay with interest.

Why should I consider a loan from the federal government?

Federal student loans usually offer borrowers lower interest rates and have more flexible repayment options than loans from banks or other private sources.

What about grants and work-study from the federal government?

This publication is focused on loans because they are the largest source of federal student aid. For detailed information on our grant and work-study programs, visit Student Aid on the Web at **www.studentaid.ed.gov/applying**. Student Aid on the Web also has information on scholarships and other sources of federal and nonfederal aid for college.

What types of federal student loans are there and how much can I borrow?

The following tables compare and summarize federal student loan programs offered by the U.S. Department of Education.

Table 2.

Federal student loan programs for the 2011–12 award year

Loan program	Eligibility (i.e., who can get the loan)	Fixed annual interest rate	Annual loan limit	Maximum loan amount allowed when you graduate	Details
Federal Perkins Loans	Undergraduate and graduate students enrolled at least part-time and who demonstrate financial need	5%	Undergraduate students: Up to $5,500 Graduate students: Up to $8,000 Amount actually received depends on financial need, amount of other aid, and availability of funds at school.	Undergraduate students: $27,500 Graduate students: $60,000 (this amount includes undergraduate loans)	Your college is the lender.
William D. Ford Direct Stafford Loans Direct Subsidized Stafford Loans	Undergraduate and graduate students enrolled at least half-time Must demonstrate financial need	Undergraduate students: For loans first disbursed on or after July 1, 2010 and before July 1, 2011: 4 5% For loans first disbursed on or after July 1, 2011 and before July 1, 2012: 3.4% Graduate students: 6.8%	$3,500–$8,500, depending on year in school A detailed breakdown is provided in Table 4.	Undergraduate students: $23,000 Graduate students: $65,500	The U.S. Department of Education is the lender and pays interest on the loan while you are in school at least half-time and during grace and deferment periods.
Direct Unsubsidized Stafford Loans	Undergraduate and graduate students enrolled at least half-time Financial need is not required	6.8%	$5,500–$20,500 (less any subsidized amount received for the same period) depending on year in school and dependency status A detailed breakdown is provided in Table 4.	Dependent undergraduate students: $31,000 (no more than $23,000 of this amount may be in subsidized loans) Independent undergraduate students: $57,500 (no more than $23,000 of this amount may be in subsidized loans) Graduate students: $138,500 (no more than $65,500 of this amount may be in subsidized loans)—this includes loans received for undergraduate study	The U.S. Department of Education is the lender. You are responsible for paying all interest on the loan starting on the date the loan is first disbursed.

Federal student loan programs for 2011–12 (continued from page 5)

Loan program	Eligibility (i.e., who can get the loan)	Fixed annual interest rate	Annual loan limit	Maximum loan amount allowed when you graduate	Details
Direct PLUS Loans	Graduate and professional students and parents of dependent undergraduate students Student must be enrolled at least half-time Financial need is not required Those qualifying must not have adverse credit history.	7 9%	The student's cost of attendance (determined by the school) minus any other financial aid received	No aggregate limit for PLUS Loans	The U.S. Department of Education is the lender. The loan is unsubsidized (i.e., you are responsible for paying all interest).
Direct Consolidation Loans	Students who want to combine multiple federal student loans into one loan Parent PLUS loans cannot be transferred to the student and become the student's responsibility.	Fixed rate is based on the weighted average of the interest rates on the loans being consolidated, rounded up to the nearest one-eighth of 1%. Cannot exceed 8 25%	Not applicable	Not applicable	

For interest rates on loans disbursed before July 1, 2010, go to **www.studentaid.ed.gov/interestrates**.

NOTE: *Before July 1, 2010, Stafford, PLUS, and Consolidation Loans also were made by private lenders under the Federal Family Education Loan (FFEL*[SM]*) Program. As a result of legislation passed in 2010, no further loans will be made under the FFEL Program. All new Stafford, PLUS, and Consolidation Loans will come directly from the U.S. Department of Education under the Direct Loan Program.*

Prepare

Because you can't borrow more than your cost of attendance minus any other financial aid you'll get, you may receive less than the annual maximum amounts. Also, the annual loan limits assume that your program of study is at least a full academic year. The maximum annual and total loan limits include any Stafford Loans you may have received under the FFEL Program.

Table 3.
Comparison of subsidized vs. unsubsidized loans: interest rates, interest accrual and payment, and capitalization

Subsidized	Unsubsidized
The federal government pays interest on subsidized loans while you are in school at least half-time and during grace and deferment periods.	Interest starts accruing (accumulating) from the time the funds are disbursed to you.
	You're responsible for paying that interest.
	You can choose to either pay it while you are in school or let it accrue.
	The amount you let accrue will be added to the principal balance of your loan (capitalized).
	If you let your interest capitalize, it increases your loan principal balance and you will then have to pay interest on the increased loan principal amount. The total amount you repay over the life of your loan will be greater than if you paid interest while you were in school.

Graduate and professional students enrolled in certain health profession programs may receive additional Unsubsidized Stafford Loan amounts beyond those shown in table 4. There is also an increased aggregate loan limit of $224,000 (maximum $65,500 subsidized).

Table 4.
Annual and aggregate loan limits for Direct Stafford Loans

Year	Dependent undergraduate students (except students whose parents are unable to obtain PLUS Loans)	Independent undergraduate students (and dependent students whose parents are unable to obtain PLUS Loans)	Graduate and professional degree students
First Year	$5,500—No more than $3,500 of this amount may be in subsidized loans.	$9,500—No more than $3,500 of this amount may be in subsidized loans.	$20,500—No more than $8,500 of this amount may be in subsidized loans.
Second Year	$6,500—No more than $4,500 of this amount may be in subsidized loans.	$10,500—No more than $4,500 of this amount may be in subsidized loans.	
Third Year and Beyond (each year)	$7,500—No more than $5,500 of this amount may be in subsidized loans.	$12,500—No more than $5,500 of this amount may be in subsidized loans.	
Maximum total debt from Direct Stafford Loans when you graduate	$31,000—No more than $23,000 of this amount may be in subsidized loans.	$57,500—No more than $23,000 of this amount may be in subsidized loans.	$138,500—No more than $65,500 of this amount may be in subsidized loans. The graduate debt limit includes Stafford Loans received for undergraduate study.

> NOTE: *If your parents don't qualify for a PLUS Loan, you might be able to get additional funds up to the amount listed under independent undergraduate students in table 2. See your financial aid administrator (FAA) for more information.*

Can I get an estimate on how much aid I will get?

Yes. *FAFSA4caster*[SM] is a calculator that you can use to get an estimate of the federal student aid (grants, work-study, and loans) you may receive. You can access *FAFSA4caster* at **www.FAFSA4caster.ed.gov** and **www.fafsa.gov**.

Do all schools participate in the federal loan programs?

No, they don't. You need to contact your school to find out if it participates in the federal loan programs.

How are federal student loans different from private loans?

While every student wants scholarships and grants, not everyone can cover the entire cost of college or career school through those options. Loans can make your education possible and affordable.

However, when exploring your loan options, you should consider federal student loans before any private loans. Federal student loans have lower and fixed interest rates, generous repayment plans, no prepayment penalties, and no credit checks (except for PLUS Loans).

In contrast, private loans, which may be aggressively marketed to students through TV ads, mailings, and other media, are substantially more expensive than federal student loans. They generally have higher, variable interest rates that may substantially increase the total amount you repay and the interest rate you receive might depend on your credit score. Private loans also can have prepayment penalty fees.

Table 5 shows why federal student loans are a better option than private student loans.

Table 5.
Federal student loans vs. private loans

Federal student loans (loans from the federal government through the U.S. Department of Education)	Private student loans (nonfederal loans from a bank, credit union, or other financial institution)
You will not have to start repaying your federal student loans until you graduate, leave school, or change your enrollment status to less than half-time (see page 24).	Many private student loans require payments while you are still in school.
The interest rate is fixed and is almost always lower than private loans—and much lower than credit card interest rates. For loans first disbursed on or after July 1, 2010, and before July 1, 2011, the interest rate is 4 5% for subsidized loans for undergraduate students and 6.8% for unsubsidized loans for undergraduate and graduate students. The rate for subsidized loans made to graduate students is 6.8%.	Private student loans can have variable interest rates, some greater than 18%.
Students with greater financial need might qualify for a subsidized loan. The government pays the interest.	Private student loans are not subsidized. No one pays the interest on your loan but you.
You don't need to pass a credit check to get a federal student loan (except for PLUS Loans). Federal student loans can help you establish a good credit record.	Private student loans may require an established credit record. The cost of a private student loan depends on your credit score, which you may not yet have as a student.
You don't need a co-signer (except for PLUS Loans) to get a federal student loan.	You may need a co-signer to get the best possible deal.
Free help is available at **1-800-4-FED-AID** and on our websites. You also have 24/7 access to your loan account information via the Internet.	You need to find out if there is free help.
Some interest is tax deductible.	Interest may not be tax deductible.
Loans can be consolidated into a Direct Consolidation Loan. See **www.loanconsolidation.ed.gov** or page 33 for more information on consolidation loans and to see if this option will benefit you.	Private student loans can't be consolidated into the federal loan consolidation program.
No prepayment penalty fee.	You need to make sure there are no prepayment penalty fees.

Also avoid using credit cards to pay for your education. Interest rates on credit cards are very high, payments are due every month, and usually don't offer different repayment and deferment (temporarily postpone payments) options.

Table 6.
Sources of financial aid

Maximize the Sources of Aid You Don't Have to Repay	
MONEY YOU DO NOT HAVE TO REPAY	1. Scholarships and Grants 2. Savings 3. Work-Study Earnings
CHEAPEST LOANS	4. Federal Student Loans • Perkins Loans • Direct Subsidized Stafford Loan • Direct Unsubsidized Stafford Loan • PLUS Loans
EXPENSIVE LOANS	5. Private Educational Loans 6. Home Equity Loans 7. Credit Cards

Source: Consumers Union. July 2007. *Helping Families Finance College: Improved Student Loan Disclosures and Counseling.* Yonkers, NY.

Plan ahead and graduate with less debt

After exploring the various non-loan and low-interest loan options, another option is to reduce your cost of attending college. You can start at a less expensive school or community college before transferring to a four-year college (make sure the four-year school you're interested in accepts course credits from the community college you're attending), and consider in-state vs. out-of-state schools. Debt adds up quickly, so keep an eye on it. If you're concerned about too much debt you can:

- search for more scholarships and grants;
- work while you're attending school;
- change your spending habits; and
- consider transferring to a less-expensive school.

Always consider what you'll have to repay and keep track of how much you're borrowing

Your student loan payments should only be a small percentage of your salary after you graduate. Ask your school's financial aid office for starting salaries of recent graduates in your field of study to get an idea of how much you are likely to earn after you graduate. Estimates of salaries for different careers are available in the Department of Labor's *Occupational Outlook Handbook* at **www.bls.gov/oco**. You also should research employment opportunities advertised in the area where you plan to live to get an idea of a local starting salary.

Manage your money and change your spending habits

Resist the urge to get a credit card or to get more than one credit card. A credit card can help you build a credit history, if you use it wisely. But use it for emergencies only and don't spend more than you can afford to pay. If you decide to get a credit card, make sure you understand the terms and read the fine print. You should also open a checking account, if you don't already have one, and learn how to balance your checkbook.

A few more tips to save money while you're in school:

- Buy used books instead of new ones whenever possible.
- Use your prepaid meal plan instead of eating out.
- Take advantage of free activities (e.g., concerts, plays, art exhibits) sponsored by your school.
- Resist impulse buying. Buy what you need, not what you think would be nice to have. When you do shop, use coupons and look for sales.
- Stay healthy to keep medical bills and loss of class time to a minimum. Prepackaged food might seem cheap, but you also can find inexpensive, fresh, and healthy foods if you plan ahead.
- Understand your cell phone plan. Stay within your free minutes. Remember that texting is usually not free.
- Brew your own coffee.

APPLY—LEARN HOW TO APPLY FOR AID

The U.S. Department of Education has billions of dollars in federal student aid to help students pay for college. But in order to potentially receive some of this money, you have to apply for it. This section provides information on who is eligible for federal student aid and the application process.

Who can get federal student aid?

Our most basic eligibility requirements are that you must

- be a U.S. citizen or eligible noncitizen,
- have a valid Social Security number,
- register (if you haven't already) with Selective Service, if you're a male between the ages of 18 and 25,
- be working toward a degree or certificate,
- maintain satisfactory academic progress once you're in a postsecondary school, and
- show you're qualified to obtain a postsecondary education.

These are general requirements. To get more detailed information, see **www.studentaid.ed.gov/eligible**.

How do I apply for federal student aid?

Fill out an application! Apply for federal student aid, including a federal student loan, by completing the *Free Application for Federal Student Aid* (FAFSA℠) at **www.fafsa.gov**. In addition to federal student loans, the FAFSA also determines your eligibility for other federal student aid (grants and work-study). Many states and schools use your FAFSA information to determine your eligibility for state and institutional aid. You must submit the FAFSA to receive federal student aid.

When should I complete the FAFSA?

Complete and submit the FAFSA at **www.fafsa.gov** on or after Jan. 1 of the year you expect to start college.

What information do I need?

Completing the FAFSA is very straightforward, but you will need some documents to assist you in filling out the form, such as your or your parent's most recent income tax return. You'll find a list of documents you need when you complete the online application at **www.fafsa.gov**.

How can I get help completing the FAFSA?

If you need help filling out the FAFSA, the online application has help text tools and a live chat option. If you'd like to talk to someone, then you can call our Federal Student Aid Information Center at **1-800-4-FED-AID (1-800-433-3243; TTY 1-800-730-8913)**.

What if I can't complete the FAFSA online?

If you can't complete the FAFSA online, you can get a paper copy by calling the Federal Student Aid Information Center at **1-800-4-FED-AID (1-800-433-3243)** or you can download a PDF at **www.fafsa.gov**. If at all possible, you should complete your FAFSA online at **www.fafsa.gov**. The online application has features that let you skip some questions if they don't apply and automatic error checking that streamlines your application process.

> NOTE: *By completing the FAFSA, you will be applying for federal grants, work-study, and loans.*

What about loans?

All students interested in federal student aid must complete the FAFSA to apply for grants, work-study, and loans.

The school's financial aid office can provide additional instructions for parents on how to apply for Federal PLUS Loans. However, dependent undergraduate students of parents applying for a PLUS Loan must complete a FAFSA.

Is our income too high to qualify for aid?

Aid is intended to make a college education a reality for as many students as possible, all of whom have many different financial situations. Complete the FAFSA, even if you don't expect to qualify for need-based grants and loans. By completing the FAFSA you'll also be considered for Direct Unsubsidized Stafford Loans, which are not based on need. Also, you can't be certain that you won't qualify for a subsidized loan and might end up missing out on the benefits of a subsidized loan.

The number of other family members in college at the time of your application is taken into consideration when your eligibility for federal student aid is calculated. In addition, when preparing your financial aid package school financial aid administrators (FAAs) often take into account not only income but other factors, such as medical expenses. Many families are surprised by the aid they can receive.

How do I apply for state and school aid?

The information you provide on your FAFSA is used to determine your eligibility for some state and institutional (school) aid. This aid is often provided on a first-come, first-served basis, so submit your FAFSA as soon as possible on or after Jan. 1 to be considered for this aid. Visit the website of each school you're interested in to learn their priority deadlines for school and state financial aid, and to find out about any special requirements, such as additional paperwork the school might need from you. Also, most colleges have deadlines for completing the FAFSA. Because some funds are limited and run out, meeting deadlines is always very important. You can also find a list of state deadlines at **www.fafsa.gov**.

I submitted my FAFSA—what happens next?

After you submit your FAFSA, we will send you a *Student Aid Report* (SAR), which is a summary of the FAFSA data you submitted. Review your SAR and, if needed, make changes or corrections and submit those changes for reprocessing. If you don't have any changes, you don't need to do anything. Your complete and correct SAR will contain your Expected Family Contribution (EFC)—the number used to determine your federal student aid eligibility during one school year. Make sure your EFC appears in your SAR.

We also send your SAR to the schools you identified on your FAFSA. From this point on, you must stay in contact with your school's financial aid office because they will put together your financial aid package.

The RECEIVE section (page 15) of this publication has additional information on next steps.

NOTES

RECEIVE—Learn When and How You Will Receive Your Aid

You completed and submitted your FAFSA, reviewed your *Student Aid Report*, made any needed changes, and made sure that your school has all your required information. So, what happens next? From now on, you'll contact your school's financial aid office to keep track of your financial aid award.

Your award letter

If you included the school on your FAFSA, the school will receive the results of your FAFSA. After you receive an admissions letter from the school, usually sent in April, its financial aid office will put together a financial aid award package for you and send you a financial aid award letter.

The award letter will explain how much and which forms of aid you've qualified for. Because your award package is tailored for you and is based on the cost of attending a particular school, aid amounts and information included will vary from school to school.

> NOTE: *Need-based financial aid takes into account the school's cost of attendance (all direct and indirect expenses, including tuition, fees, room and board, books, transportation, and supplies) minus the EFC (an index used to determine your financial aid eligibility).*

Evaluate your award

The award letter describes the aid you are offered. Although it's individually tailored, you're not obligated to accept all of the aid or to borrow the full amount of any loans listed in the award letter. It's up to you and your family to evaluate the award, compare it to awards from other schools, and then decide what to accept and how much to borrow. Read your award letter carefully. Loans can be classified in many ways but you should be able to tell if you're getting a subsidized or unsubsidized loan. If you have any questions or don't understand what's in your award letter, contact the school. The school also will tell you what actions you need to take after you review your award letter. Always ask questions and be an informed borrower. Make sure you understand what you're receiving and the repayment terms.

Before you accept any aid you need more information

- Get a breakdown of the direct expenses (tuition, room and board, and fees) and estimates of indirect expenses (travel, books, etc.) for one year of college;
- Know the actual amount (cost of attendance minus financial aid) that you'll have to pay to attend one year of college;

- Know how much in scholarships and grants (money that doesn't have to be repaid) you've been awarded, the conditions under which they are renewable each year, and any other conditions you must meet to receive these funds;
- Know the exact amount of work-study you've been awarded and the conditions to fulfill the work-study requirements;
- Find out which types of loans you've been awarded and the amounts;
- Find out which federal loans your parents can get to help pay for your education;
- Know the interest rates, loan terms, monthly repayment amounts, and total repayment amounts of your loans;
- Know where you can get additional information or have your loan questions answered; and
- Make sure you understand the source of your loan (government or private) and the terms of the loan and only consider those with the most favorable terms.

> NOTE: *Documents for federal student loans will state somewhere on the form that it is a federal student loan. Some private student loan lenders have forms that look similar to the federal forms. Make sure what you're getting is, in fact, a federal student loan.*

Is your family's share of college costs still more than you can afford? If so, you may want to consider the Direct Unsubsidized Loans listed in your letter. These federal loans offer more favorable terms than private and commercial loans (see page 9).
If you're a dependent student, your parents can apply for a PLUS Loan (see page 6).

Try other free sources of information to ensure you have considered all viable options for securing adequate, yet the least costly, financial aid, such as your state education agency, the financial aid office at the school you plan on attending, professional organizations, etc. For more sources of information, go to *Looking for Student Aid* at **www.studentaid.ed.gov/LSA.**

> NOTE: *Your award letter or financial aid package doesn't transfer with you if you go to another school. Contact the financial aid office at your new school as early as possible to find out what to do.*

Accepting the loan offered to you

Accepting a loan listed in the award letter involves some additional steps, which vary depending on the type of loan you're receiving. Saying yes is as simple as signing a promissory note (a contract between you and the U.S. Department of Education that specifies terms and conditions of the loan). By signing the promissory note, you are promising to repay your student loan. The financial aid office will guide you through the paperwork or direct you to **www.studentloans.gov** to sign the online Master

Promissory Note (MPN). The MPN is a legal document in which the borrower promises to repay the loan and any accrued interest and fees to the U.S. Department of Education. The MPN can cover multiple academic years. Contact the financial aid administrator at your school if you need more information or have any questions about your award letter.

When you obtain a federal student loan, you have certain responsibilities. Consider the following important responsibilities regarding your loan:

Think about how much you're borrowing

- Accept scholarships and grants you're eligible for and understand the conditions you must meet.
- Accept the loans with the most favorable terms; that is, federal student loans and state aid offered to you (see page 9). If you see private or commercial loans in your award letter, ask why this type of loan was included, find out the terms, and reject the private loan if the terms aren't favorable.
- Borrow only what you need. If you don't repay your student loan on time or according to the terms in your promissory note, you could default on this legal obligation, which has serious consequences and will adversely affect your credit rating, and make any future lending much more difficult if not impossible.

Signing a promissory note means you agree to repay the loan

- When you sign a promissory note, you're agreeing to repay the loan according to the terms of the note. Be sure to read your promissory note.
- The note states that you must repay the loan unless you meet the requirements for loan discharge (cancellation), even if you don't complete your education.
- Also, you **must** repay your loan even if you can't get a job after you complete the program or you didn't like the education you received. The U.S. Department of Education does not guarantee the quality of education you receive or that you will find a job in your field of study.

Make payments regardless of receiving billing notices

- You must make payments on your loan even if you don't receive a bill or repayment notice.
- Billing statements (or coupon books) are sent to you as a convenience. You're obligated to make payments even if you don't receive any reminders.
- You also must make monthly payments in the full amount required by your repayment plan, in order to keep your account in good standing. Partial payments do not fulfill your obligation to repay your student loan on time.

Receive entrance and exit counseling

- If you are a first-time borrower you must complete an **entrance counseling** session before you're given your first loan disbursement. This session provides you with useful tips and tools to help you develop a budget for managing your education expenses and helps you to understand your loan responsibilities. Parent PLUS Loan borrowers do not participate in entrance counseling.

- You must receive **exit counseling** before you leave school to make sure you understand your rights and responsibilities as a borrower. You will receive information about repayment and your loan servicer will notify you of the date loan repayment begins (usually six months after you graduate, leave school, or drop below half-time enrollment). Parent PLUS Loan borrowers do not participate in exit counseling.

When to notify your loan servicer

Notify your loan servicer of your enrollment status when you

- graduate;
- withdraw from school;
- drop below half-time status;
- change your name, address, or Social Security number (new Social Security numbers are issued only in very rare circumstances; see **www.ssa.gov/ssnumber** for rules on changing them), or
- transfer to another school.

How and when do I receive the money from my federal student loans?

There are a few things to remember:

- Funds will be sent directly to the school in two disbursements (installments). No disbursement will be greater than half the amount of your loan.
- If you're a first-year undergraduate student and a first-time borrower, you must complete entrance counseling and your first disbursement can't be made until 30 days after the first day of your enrollment period.
- Your school usually credits your loan payment to school charges on your account (tuition and fees, room and board, and other authorized charges).
- If the loan money exceeds your school charges, the school will pay you the credit balance by check or other means.

What can I use my federal student loan money for?

You may use the money you receive only to pay for education expenses at the school that awarded your loan. Education expenses include such school charges as tuition, room and board, fees, books, supplies, equipment, dependent child care expenses, transportation, and rental or purchase of a personal computer. Talk to someone at the financial aid office at your school if you need more details.

What is interest?

Interest is a loan expense charged by the lender and paid by the borrower for the use of borrowed money. The expense is calculated as a percentage of the unpaid principal amount (loan amount), which includes the original amount borrowed and any capitalized interest.

What is the interest rate on my federal student loan?

Fixed interest rates for Direct Subsidized Loans for undergraduate borrowers are

- 4.5% for loans first disbursed on or after July 1, 2010 and before July 1, 2011.
- 3.4% for loans first disbursed on or after July 1, 2011 and before July 1, 2012.
- 6.8% for loans first disbursed on or after July 1, 2012.

The interest rates for Direct Subsidized Loans for graduate students and Direct Unsubsidized Loans for undergraduate and graduate students is 6.8%. For Direct PLUS Loans, the interest rate is 7.9%.

For detailed information on interest rates, go to **www.studentaid.ed.gov/interestrates**.

Interest rate cap for military members

If you qualify under the *Service Members Civil Relief Act*, the interest rate on loans you obtained before entering military service may be capped at 6% during your military service. You must contact your loan servicer to request this benefit.

In addition, the U.S. Department of Education does not charge interest (for a period of no more than 60 months) on Direct Loans first disbursed on or after Oct. 1, 2008, while you are serving on active duty or performing qualifying National Guard duty during a war or other military operation or other emergency, and serving in an area of hostilities qualifying for special pay.

Isn't my interest subsidized (paid) by the government?

Depending on the type of federal student loan you have, the interest is either paid by you (unsubsidized loan) or by the federal government (subsidized loan). See page 7 for more information on unsubsidized and subsidized loans.

Who sets interest rates for federal student loans?

Interest rates on federal student loans are set by Congress.

How is interest calculated?

The amount of interest that accrues on your loan from month to month is determined by a Simple Daily Interest formula. This formula consists of multiplying your loan balance by the number of days since the last payment times the Interest Rate Factor (see more on interest rate factor on next page).

Monthly interest can be calculated using this Simple Daily Interest formula:

| Number of days since last payment | x | Principal balance outstanding (PBO) | x | Interest rate factor | = | Interest amount |

Interest rate factor

The interest rate factor is used to calculate the amount of interest that accrues on your loan. It is determined by dividing your loan's interest rate by 365.25 (the number of days in a year). See table 7 for some examples of interest rate factors.

Table 7.
Calculation of interest rate factor, by select interest rates

Interest rate	Converted to decimals	Divided by 365.25	Interest rate factor
8 99%	.0899	.0899/ 365.25	.00024613
8 25%	.0825	.0825/ 365.25	.00022587
7 59%	.0759	.0759/ 365.25	.00020780

Note: 365.25 is the number of days in a year.

Practice Example: Let's say the remaining balance on your loan is $9,500 and your interest rate is 8.25% (interest rate factor is .00022587). You sent in a payment of $160 32 days after your previous month's payment, and you're wondering how much of that payment went toward the principal balance of your loan.

> 32 (days) x $9,500.00 (PBO) x .00022587 (interest rate factor) = $68.66 of your payment applied to interest
>
> $160.00 (payment) − $68.66 (interest) = $91 34 applied to your principal loan balance

In this scenario, you paid $68.66 toward interest and $91.34 toward the principal balance. This would leave you with a principal loan balance of $9,408.66 after the $160.00 payment was applied ($9,500.00 PBO − $91.34 paid toward PBO = new PBO of $9,408.66).

Go to **www.studentaid.ed.gov/repaying** or contact your loan servicer for more information.

Are there any other fees?

All loans have loan fees (also called origination fees) that are deducted proportionately from each loan disbursement you receive. This means the money you receive will be less than the amount you actually borrow. You're responsible for repaying the entire amount you borrowed and not just the amount you received in loan disbursements. The loan fee for Direct Stafford Loans first disbursed on or after July 1, 2010, is 1%. The Direct PLUS Loan fee is 4%.

> NOTE: *Interest is charged on PLUS Loans during ALL periods, beginning on the date of the first loan disbursement. A PLUS borrower may pay the interest as it accrues during a deferment, or allow it to accrue and be capitalized at the end of the deferment period.*

I don't need to borrow all this money. What should I do?

You can notify your school before your loan is disbursed that you don't need to borrow all or part of your loan and within certain time frames after your loan has been disbursed. The time frames and the procedures for canceling a loan, also are explained in notices that the school is required to send you. Contact your financial aid office for more details.

Loans add up! Watch your finances carefully!

Loans accumulate over the two, four, five years or more that you will attend school. Estimating the full cost of attendance for the total number of years you plan to attend school will help you understand how much you may have to borrow. Once you have an idea of the total amount of federal student loans you may be taking out, you can see how much your monthly payments could be. See estimated monthly payment amounts for different repayment plans, see pages 27–28.

Keep track of how much you're borrowing

To keep track of all your U.S. Department of Education loans, access the National Student Loan Data System℠ (NSLDS℠) at **www.nslds.ed.gov**, the central database for federal student aid. You'll need to use your PIN to access your information.

Keep good records. Repaying your student loan(s) is a very serious matter, and it's important to keep accurate, accessible records. You should set up a file folder for each loan and file all paperwork. Your file should include:

- Financial aid award letters;
- Loan counseling materials (entrance and exit counseling);
- Promissory note(s);
- Amount of your student loans, including the amount that is disbursed each semester or year (you may access this information at **www.nslds.ed.gov**);
- Account numbers for each of your loans;
- Name, address, phone number, and website of your loan servicer (the entity to whom you send your monthly payments);
- Loan disclosure and payment schedule sent to you by your servicer before you start to repay your loan;
- Monthly payment stubs (if you pay by check) or printouts of proof of payment (if you pay electronically);
- Notes about any questions you ask about your loans, the answers, and the name of the person to whom you spoke;
- Any deferment or forbearance paperwork and notes of any phone calls to the servicer; and
- Documentation proving that you paid your loans in full.

Receive

What if I need to take a break from school or I just can't go full-time?

If you're preparing to leave school, withdraw early, or transfer to another school, you must remember to notify your loan servicer and the school you're currently attending of the change in your enrollment status.

When your enrollment status changes, there are a few steps that you must take to ensure your loans are processed correctly.

Table 8.
Change in enrollment status: Steps to ensure correct loan processing, by status change

Status change	Steps to take					
	Contact financial aid office	Complete exit counseling	Notify loan servicer	Begin loan repayment after your grace period	Apply for financial aid by completing the FAFSA	Request an in-school deferment
Withdraw from school	X	X	X	X		
Drop your enrollment to less than half-time	X	X	X	X		
Return to school at least half-time after a period of less than half-time				X	X	X
Transfer to another school	X	X		X	X	X
Graduate		X		X		
Go to graduate school				X	X	X

NOTE: *Before July 1, 2010, Stafford, PLUS, and Consolidation Loans were also made by private lenders under the Federal Family Education Loan (FFEL^SM) Program. As a result of recent legislation, no further loans will be made under the FFEL Program. All new Stafford, PLUS, and Consolidation Loans will come directly from the U.S. Department of Education under the Direct Loan Program.*

Receive

REPAY—LEARN ABOUT THE REPAYMENT PROCESS AND OPTIONS

If you have a federal student loan, you pay lower interest rates than you would on a commercial loan because the federal government subsidizes federal loans. You also don't have to begin to repay most federal student loans until you leave school or drop below half-time. As generous as these terms are, you need to remember that you have to repay your loan. Failure to do so could result in your loan(s) being declared delinquent or in default and can have a negative impact on your credit score. This section outlines repayment requirements and describes the rare circumstances under which your obligation to repay can be reduced or forgiven.

What you need to know

You have the right to detailed information about your loan.

Know the details of your loan

Below is what you need to know and must receive from your school or loan servicer:

- information about the yearly and total amounts you can borrow;
- the amount of your total debt (principal and estimated interest), your current interest rate and the total interest charges on your loan;
- the date you must start repayment;
- a complete list of any charges you must pay (loan fees) and information on how those charges are collected;
- information about the maximum repayment periods and the minimum repayment amount;
- a current description of your loans, including average anticipated monthly payments;
- the name of the loan servicer that holds your loans, where to send your payments and where to write or call if you have questions;
- an explanation of the fees you might be charged during the repayment period, such as late charges and collection or litigation costs if you're delinquent or in default;
- an explanation of default and its consequences;
- a reminder of available options for loan consolidation;
- a reminder that you can prepay your loan in whole or in part without penalty at any time;

- a description of applicable deferment, forbearance, and discharge (cancellation) provisions;

- repayment options and advice about debt management that will help you in making your payments;

- notification that you must provide your expected permanent address and the name and address of your expected employer; and

- notification that you must provide any corrections to your school's records concerning your name, Social Security number, references, and driver's license number (if you have one).

You must have access to your loan repayment schedule

Your loan servicer must give you a loan repayment schedule that states:

- when your first payment is due;

- the number and frequency of payments; and

- the amount of each payment.

You will be notified if your loan servicer changes

You must be notified if your loan servicer changes and if it results in making payments to a new servicer. You must be given:

- the identity of the new loan servicer; and

- the address where you or your parents must send payments, and the telephone numbers of both the old and new loan servicer.

When do I repay my loans?

Federal student loans have grace periods. There is a set period of time after you graduate, leave school, or drop below half-time status before you must begin repayment on a Direct or FFEL Stafford or Perkins Loan. This period of time is called a grace period and gives you time to get financially settled and select your repayment plan. Not all federal student loans have the same grace period (see below).

- **Federal Perkins Loans**—the grace period is nine months. However, if you're attending less than half-time, check with your financial aid office to determine your grace period. During the grace period, you don't have to pay any principal, and you won't be charged interest.

- **Direct or FFEL Stafford Loans**—the grace period is six months.

  ▶ **Subsidized loan**—during the grace period, you don't have to pay any principal, and you won't be charged interest.

  ▶ **Unsubsidized loan**—you don't have to pay any principal, but you will be charged interest. Remember, you can either pay the interest as you go along or it will be capitalized (i.e., added to the principal loan balance) later.

- **Direct or FFEL PLUS Loans**—the repayment period for a PLUS loan begins on the date the loan is fully disbursed as there is no grace period.

Repay

- Graduate and professional student PLUS borrowers may defer repayment while they are enrolled in school at least half-time and (for PLUS loans first disbursed on or after July 1, 2008) for six months after they are no longer enrolled at least half-time.

- Parent PLUS borrowers whose loans were first disbursed on or after July 1, 2008, may defer repayment while the dependent student for whom they borrowed is enrolled at least half-time and for six months after the student ceases to be enrolled at least half-time. A parent borrower who is also a student may defer repayment while he or she is enrolled at least half-time.

If you are called to active military duty for more than 30 days, the grace period will be delayed.

Repayment options

When do I choose a repayment plan?

Your loan servicer will send you information about repayment, and you'll be notified of the date repayment begins. **However, you're responsible for beginning repayment on time even if you don't receive this information.** Failing to make payments on your loan can lead to default.

There are several repayment plans to help you manage this important financial responsibility. The repayment plans outlined in table 9 are for Direct and FFEL Stafford Loans and PLUS Loans. You can change plans to suit your financial circumstances.

Federal Perkins Loans have different repayment options. Your payment depends on the amount that you borrow, but the minimum is $40 per month. Check with your school for more information on Perkins Loan repayment plans.

Table 9.
Types of repayment plans for Direct and FFEL Stafford Loans and PLUS Loans

Repayment plan	Eligible loans	Repayment time frame	Monthly payment	Additional considerations
Standard	Direct Stafford, FFEL Stafford, PLUS Loans for Parents, PLUS Loans for Graduate and Professional Students	Fixed payment for up to 10 years Up to 30 years for consolidation loans	Fixed Payment must be at least $50 per month.	If you do not choose a repayment plan when you first begin repayment, you will be placed in this one.
Graduated	Direct Stafford, FFEL Stafford, PLUS Loans for Parents, PLUS Loans for Graduate and Professional Students	Up to 10 years Up to 30 years for consolidation loans	Payments start out relatively low at first and then increase, usually every two years. Payments must at least cover the interest that accumulates on the loans between payments.	The plan is tailored to individuals with relatively low current incomes (e.g., recent college graduates) who expect their incomes to increase in the future. You'll ultimately pay more for your loan than under the Standard Plan, because more interest accumulates in the early years of the plan when the outstanding loan balance is higher.

(Continued on next page)

Repay

Table 9.

Types of repayment plans (continued from page 25)

Repayment plan	Eligible loans	Repayment time frame	Monthly payment	Additional considerations
Extended	Direct Stafford, FFEL Stafford, PLUS Loans for Parents, PLUS Loans for Graduate and Professional Students	25 years	Fixed or graduated Monthly payment is lower than it would be under the Standard Plan.	FFEL borrowers must have more than $30,000 in outstanding FFEL Program loans. Direct Loan borrowers must have more than $30,000 in outstanding Direct Loans. This means, for example, that if there is $35,000 in outstanding FFEL Program loans and $10,000 in outstanding Direct Loans, the extended repayment plan is for the FFEL Program loans, but not for the balance on the Direct Loans. For both programs, the borrower must also be a "new borrower" as of Oct. 7, 1998. You'll ultimately pay more for the loan because of the interest that accumulates during the longer repayment period.
Income-Sensitive Repayment Plan	FFEL Loans only	The maximum repayment period is 10 years	Monthly loan payment is based on annual income. As income increases or decreases, so do payments.	
Income-Contingent Repayment Plan (ICR)	Direct Stafford and Direct PLUS Loans only Direct Loan parent PLUS borrowers are not eligible for the ICR repayment plan	Have 25 years to repay under this plan; unpaid portion will be forgiven	Monthly payments will be based on annual income (and that of spouse, if married), family size, and the total amount of Direct Loans.	You may have to pay income tax on the amount that is forgiven.
Income-Based Repayment (IBR)	Direct and FFEL Stafford Loans, Direct and FFEL PLUS Loans made to students Parent PLUS Loans (or consolidation loans that repaid parent PLUS Loans) are not eligible	Have 25 years to repay under this plan; unpaid portion will be forgiven	Monthly payments are capped at 15% of discretionary income (the difference between Adjusted Gross Income and 150% of the poverty guideline for your family size and state of residence). You must have partial financial hardship to enroll in the IBR Plan. If you are married AND file taxes separately, only your income will be considered when calculating your BR payment amount.	You may have to pay income tax on the amount that is forgiven. Contact the servicer for more information on the IBR Plan.

Repay

For more information on these repayment plans and to use our interactive calculators, go to **www.studentaid.ed.gov/repaying**.

NOTE: *Federal student loans have to be repaid after you graduate, leave school, or stop attending at least half-time (see page 22 for details).*

Making your monthly payments

Estimated monthly payments for Direct and FFEL Stafford Loans and PLUS Loans

Table 10 shows estimated monthly payments for various loan amounts under each repayment plan and assumes that the student is making regular monthly payments on any unsubsidized loans and is not capitalizing the interest while in school. If the interest is capitalized (added to the outstanding principal balance), the cumulative payments and total interest charges will be higher than shown in the chart.

Table 10.

Examples of typical Direct and FFEL Stafford Loan and PLUS Loan repayment plans, by initial amount of debt and type of repayment plan

	Repayment plans									
Initial debt when you enter repayment	Standard (not to exceed 10 years)		Extended		Graduated (not to exceed 10 years)		Income Contingent (income = $25,000) for Direct Loans only			
							Single		Married/HOH	
	Per month	Total repaid	Per month	Total repaid	Per month	Total repaid	Per month	Total repaid	Per month	Total repaid
$ 3,500	$ 50	$ 4,471	Not available for this loan amount		$ 25	$ 5,157	$ 27	$ 6,092	$ 25	$ 6,405
5,000	58	6,905	Not available for this loan amount		40	7,278	38	8,703	36	9,150
7,500	83	10,357	Not available for this loan amount		59	10,919	57	13,055	54	13,725
10,500	121	14,500	Not available for this loan amount		83	15,283	80	18,277	76	19,215
15,000	173	20,714	Not available for this loan amount		119	21,834	114	26,110	108	27,451
40,000	460	55,239	$ 277	$ 83,289	316	58,229	253	72,717	197	84,352

Note: **Interest rate:** payments are calculated using the fixed interest rate of 6.8%.

Graduated repayment plan: an estimated monthly repayment amount for the first two years of the term and total loan payment. The monthly repayment amount will generally increase every two years, based on this plan.

Income-Contingent Repayment plan: assumes a 5% annual growth (Census Bureau) and calculated using the formula requirements in effect during 2006.

HOH is head of household: assumes a family size of two.

Repay

Under the Income-Based Repayment (IBR) Plan, the amount an eligible borrower would repay each month is based on the borrower's Adjusted Gross Income (AGI) and family size. The annual IBR repayment amount is 15 percent of the difference between the borrower's AGI and 150 percent of the Department of Health and Human Services most recently published poverty guidelines, adjusted for family size. That amount is then divided by 12 to get the monthly IBR payment amount.

After the initial determination of your eligibility for IBR, your payment may be adjusted each year based on your income and family size, but your required payment will never be more than the standard 10-year payment amount (unless you choose to exit the IBR program).

Table 11.
Income-Based Repayment (IBR) Plan maximum monthly payment by sample income and family size

Annual income	Family size=Number of family members						
	1	2	3	4	5	6	7
$10,000	$0	$0	$0	$0	$0	$0	$0
$15,000	$0	$0	$0	$0	$0	$0	$0
$20,000	$47	$0	$0	$0	$0	$0	$0
$25,000	$109	$39	$0	$0	$0	$0	$0
$30,000	$172	$102	$32	$0	$0	$0	$0
$35,000	$234	$164	$94	$24	$0	$0	$0
$40,000	$297	$227	$157	$87	$16	$0	$0
$45,000	$359	$289	$219	$149	$79	$9	$0
$50,000	$422	$352	$282	$212	$141	$71	$1
$55,000	$484	$414	$344	$274	$204	$134	$64
$60,000	$547	$477	$407	$337	$266	$196	$126
$65,000	$609	$539	$469	$399	$329	$259	$189
$70,000	$672	$602	$532	$462	$391	$321	$251

For more information on repayment plans and to use our calculators go to **www.studentaid.ed.gov/repaying**.

Discounts for electronic payments

You might be able get a 0.25% rate discount as a repayment incentive for automatic payments. This interest rate reduction is for having payments electronically debited from your bank account and is a rebate given up front. When you make your payments on time you are taking steps toward building a solid credit history.

To whom do I make my loan payments?

You will make loan payments to your loan servicer. When you first receive a loan, you will be contacted by the servicer for that loan. Your loan servicer will provide regular updates on the status of your loan, and any additional loans that you receive.

The U.S. Department of Education uses several loan servicers for the Direct Loan Program and for FFEL Program Loans purchased by the Department. You will be notified by the servicer on where and when to send payments and the servicer will provide you with their contact information. Because the servicer is handling the day-to-day operations of your loan, and not providing the loan funds, correspondence you receive vary from servicer to servicer.

If you can't find your servicer information or have questions about your loans, you can look up your federal student loan history through the U.S. Department of Education's National Student Loan Data System (NSLDS) at **www.nslds.ed.gov**. You will need your Federal Student Aid PIN to access the database. You also can call the Federal Student Aid Information Center at **1-800-4-FED-AID (1-800-433-3243, TTY 1-800-730-8913)**.

What if I can't make my monthly payments?

Your student loan debt is a legal obligation and can be a 10- to 30-year financial commitment.

Don't ignore debt. It won't go away.

There are many ways to get help if you are struggling, including changing your payment due date, switching repayment plans, and asking about deferment or forbearance.

If you can't make your payments, don't ignore the problem.

- Contact the servicer immediately to discuss options.
- Consider changing your repayment plan if your current one is not favorable.
- Keep track of all communications. Using the sample log below is one way to help you stay organized and on track.

Example of information to include in a communication log with your loan servicer
Date:
Servicer:
Phone number or e-mail:
Person you spoke to:
Reason you called:
Were your questions answered or issues resolved?
What were the answers to your questions?
Follow-up actions:

Why is missing a payment a problem?

Your credit history will be affected if you do not repay your loans.

If you don't make a payment on time or if you start missing payments—even one—your loan is considered delinquent and late fees can be assessed. If you are making late or partial payments, contact your loan servicer immediately for help. If you don't make payments for more than 270 days (except for Perkins Loans), your loan will go into default and your credit rating could suffer. If your credit rating is affected negatively, you may be denied future education or consumer loans, and you may not be able, for example, to obtain a mortgage, rent an apartment, buy a car, or secure employment.

What is deferment?

A deferment is a period in which repayment of the principal balance is temporarily postponed (no payments are required) if you meet certain requirements. During a deferment, if your loan is

- **Subsidized**—the government pays the interest on your loan.
- **Unsubsidized (which includes all PLUS loans)**—you are responsible for the interest that accrues during the deferment period. If you do not make any interest payments during the deferment period, the unpaid interest will be capitalized (added to the principal balance) at the end of the deferment period.

How do I get a deferment?

You have to apply for a deferment to your loan servicer, and you must continue to make payments until you've been notified your deferment has been granted. Otherwise, you could become delinquent or go into default. The most common loan deferment conditions are enrollment in school at least half-time, inability to find full-time employment (for up to three years), economic hardship (for up to three years), and military service (see next question).

Can I get a deferment while in military service?

An active duty military deferment is available to borrowers in the FFEL, Direct Loan, and Perkins Loan programs who are called to active duty during a war or other military operation or national emergency. This deferment is available:

- While you are serving in active duty during a war or other military operation or national emergency or
- While you perform qualifying National Guard duty during a war or other military operation or national emergency, or
- If you were serving on or after Oct. 1, 2007, for an additional 180-day period following the demobilization date for the qualifying service.

If you are a member of the National Guard or other reserve component of the U.S. Armed Forces (current or retired) and are called or ordered to active duty while enrolled at least half-time at an eligible school or within six months of having been enrolled at least half-time, you are eligible for a deferment during the 13 months following the conclusion of the active duty service, or until you return to enrolled student status on at least a half-time basis, whichever is earlier. Once you return to school at least half-time, your military deferment ends and you can get an in-school deferment.

Can parents or graduate and professional degree students defer repayment of their PLUS Loan?

Yes. Generally, the same deferment provisions that apply to Stafford Loans apply to PLUS Loans. Because PLUS Loans are unsubsidized, **parents and graduate and professional degree students will be charged interest during periods of deferment**. If they don't pay the interest as it accrues, it will be capitalized (added to their outstanding principal balance). Parent PLUS borrowers may defer repayment of PLUS Loans first disbursed on or after July 1, 2008, while the student for whom the loan was obtained is enrolled at least half-time, and for an additional six months after the student ceases to be enrolled at least half-time.

The conditions that must be met under Stafford and Perkins loans to qualify for a deferment are listed in table 12. For information on deferments for loans, contact your loan servicer.

If you do not meet the requirements for a deferment, you may still be eligible for forbearance.

Table 12.
Summary of loan deferment conditions for Stafford and Perkins Loans borrowers

Deferment Condition	Stafford Loans		Perkins Loans
	Direct Loans **	FFEL Loans ª	
At least half-time study at a postsecondary school	YES	YES	YES
Study in an approved graduate fellowship program or in an approved rehabilitation training program for the disabled	YES	YES	YES
Unable to find full-time employment	Up to 3 Years	Up to 3 Years	Up to 3 Years
Economic hardship (includes Peace Corps Service)	Up to 3 Years	Up to 3 Years	Up to 3 Years
Service listed under discharge/cancellation conditions	NO	NO	YES
Borrower is on active military duty during a war or other military operation or national emergency and if the borrower was serving on or after Oct. 1, 2007, for an additional 180-day period following the demobilization date for the qualifying service	YES	YES	YES
For a borrower who is a member of the National Guard or other reserve component of the U.S. Armed Forces (current or retired) and is called or ordered to active duty while enrolled at least half-time at an eligible school or within six months of having been enrolled at least half-time, during the 13 months following the conclusion of the active duty service, or until the borrower returns to enrolled student status on at least a half-time basis, whichever is earlier	YES	YES	YES

ª For PLUS Loans and unsubsidized Stafford Loans, only principal is deferred. Interest continues to accrue.

ᵇ A Direct Loan borrower who had an outstanding balance on a FFEL Loan first disbursed before July 1, 1993, when the borrower received his or her first Direct Loan, is eligible for additional deferments.

More information on teaching and other types of service deferments and cancellations can be found online at **www.studentaid.ed.gov**.

> NOTE: *You MUST continue making payments on your student loan until you have been notified that your request for deferment has been granted. If you don't, and your deferment is not approved, you will become delinquent and may default on your loan.*

What is forbearance?

Forbearance allows you to postpone or reduce your monthly payment amount for a limited and specific period if you are willing but unable to make your scheduled loan payments for reasons including, but not limited to, financial hardship or illness and you do not meet the eligibility requirements for deferment. During forbearance, for all types of loans

- You are responsible for paying the interest that accrues during forbearance on *all* loan types, including subsidized loans.
- When you resume making payments at the end of the forbearance period, any unpaid interest will be capitalized (added to the principal balance).

Your servicer is required to grant you forbearance under certain conditions. These include, but are not limited to, the following

- While you are serving in a medical or dental internship or residency program and meet certain other requirements.
- If you are having payments being made for you by the Department of Defense.
- While you are serving in an AmeriCorps position for which you are receiving an education award.
- If the total amount you owe each month on all of your FFEL, Direct, and Perkins loans is 20% or more of your total monthly gross income.

You must request forbearance and, in some cases, must provide documentation showing that you meet the eligibility requirements. Contact your servicer to request forbearance and for a complete list of forbearance and eligibility criteria.

> **Important!** *Continue making payments on your loan while you're waiting for deferment or forbearance approval. You must continue to make payments until you have been notified that your request has been approved. Keep a copy of any request form you submit, and document all contact you have with the loan servicer.*

For more information on deferment or forbearance go to **www.studentaid.ed.gov/repaying** and click on "Difficulty Repaying."

Consolidation loans

What is loan consolidation?

Student and parent borrowers can consolidate (combine) multiple federal student loans with various repayment schedules into one Direct Consolidation Loan. The result is a single monthly payment instead of multiple monthly payments.

With a consolidation loan:

- Your monthly payment might be lower.
- Your repayment period may be extended up to 30 years (depending on the amount of your consolidation loan and your other student loan debt).

Carefully review your consolidation options before you apply. Talk to your loan servicer for more information before you consolidate.

If you're in default on a federal student loan, you still might be able to consolidate if you make satisfactory repayment arrangements on the defaulted loan or agree to repay the consolidation loan under the Income-Contingent, Income-Sensitive, or Income-Based Repayment Plans, provided the defaulted loan is not subject to a judgment or wage garnishment.

What kinds of loans can be consolidated?

All federal student loans discussed in this guide are eligible for consolidation. To get a complete list of your loans that are eligible for consolidation, contact your loan servicer.

When can I consolidate my loans?

For both FFEL and Direct Loans you can consolidate:

- During your grace period.
- Once you've entered repayment (the day after the end of the six-month grace period).
- During periods of deferment or forbearance.

What's the interest rate on a consolidation loan?

The interest rate is a fixed rate for the life of the loan. The fixed rate is based on the weighted average of the interest rates on all of the loans you consolidate, rounded up to the nearest one-eighth of 1 percent. The interest rate will never exceed 8.25%.

Are there any disadvantages to getting a consolidation loan?

Yes, there could be. For example, consolidation may significantly increase the total cost of repaying your loans. Because you may have a longer period of time to repay (up to 30 years), you'll pay more interest. Compare the cost of repaying your unconsolidated loans with the cost of repaying a consolidation loan. Things to consider are:

- Whether you'll lose any borrower benefits if you consolidate, such as interest rate discounts or principal rebates, as these benefits can significantly reduce the cost of repaying your loans.

- If you include a Perkins Loan in your Consolidation Loan, you will lose cancellation benefits that are only available in the Perkins Loan Program.

How do I get a consolidation loan and where can I get more information?

Contact Direct Loan Consolidation at **1-800-557-7392**, or go to **www.loanconsolidation.ed.gov**. TTY users may call **1-800-557-7395**.

Loan cancellation

Is it ever possible to have my federal student loan canceled?

Under certain specific circumstances, you can have all or part of your loan canceled or discharged. For more information, go to **www.studentaid.ed.gov/discharges**.

In certain cases, you may be able to have all or a part of your loan canceled because:

- Your school closed before you completed your program.

- Your school forged your signature on your promissory note or falsely certified that you were eligible to get the loan.

- Your loan was falsely certified because of identity theft (additional requirements apply).

- You withdrew from school, but the school didn't pay a refund that it owed under its written policy or the U.S. Department of Education's regulations. Check with the school to see how refund policies apply to federal aid at the school.

- Your loan was canceled in bankruptcy claim. This is not an automatic process— you must prove to the bankruptcy court that repaying the loan would cause undue hardship.

- If you are a teacher and also a new borrower (i.e., you did not have an outstanding balance on an FFEL or Direct Loan on Oct. 1, 1998, or on the date you obtained an FFEL or Direct Loan after Oct. 1, 1998) and have been teaching full-time in a low-income elementary or secondary school or educational service agency for five consecutive years, you may be able to have as much as $17,500 of your subsidized or unsubsidized loans canceled. This provision is not available for borrowers of PLUS Loans. For more information visit **www.studentaid.ed.gov/tc** or call the Direct Loan Servicing Center at **1-800-848-0979**. For teacher cancellation under the Perkins Loan program see table 13 on page 35.

- If you are employed in certain public service jobs and have made 120 payments on your Direct Loans (after Oct. 1, 2007), the remaining balance that you owe may be forgiven. Only payments made under certain repayment plans may be counted toward the required 120 payments. You must not be in default on the loans that are forgiven. For more information, go to **www.studentaid.ed.gov** and click on Public Service Loan Forgiveness.

Total and permanent disability and student death

Your loan may be discharged if you are determined to be totally and permanently disabled. Totally and permanently disabled is the condition of an individual who is unable to engage in any substantial gainful activity by reason of any medically determinable physical or mental impairment that can be expected to result in death; has lasted for a continuous period of not less than 60 months; or can be expected to last for a continuous period of not less than 60 months; or has been determined by the Secretary of Veterans Affairs to be unemployable due to a service-connected disability. To apply for this discharge, a physician must certify the discharge application. For more information, go to **www.disabilitydischarge.com**.

For a student who dies, the loan will be canceled if a family member or other representative provides an original or a copy of the original or certified copy of the death certificate.

Lists of discharge and cancellation provisions for Perkins Loans and Stafford and PLUS loans are found in tables 13 and 14, respectively. For a complete list on loan discharges go to **www.studentaid.ed.gov/discharges** or contact your loan servicer.

Table 13.
Perkins loan cancellation/discharge and percentage forgiven

Conditions	Percentage of amount forgiven
Bankruptcy (in rare cases—cancellation is possible only if the bankruptcy court rules that repayment would cause undue hardship)	100 percent
Closed school (before student could complete program of study)—applies to loans received on or after Jan. 1, 1986	100 percent
Borrower's total and permanent disability or death	100 percent
Full-time teacher in a designated elementary or secondary school serving students from low-income families	100 percent
Full-time special education teacher (includes teaching children with disabilities in a public or other nonprofit elementary or secondary school)	Up to 100 percent
Full-time qualified professional provider of early intervention services for the disabled	Up to 100 percent
Full-time teacher of math, science, foreign languages, bilingual education, or other fields designated as teacher shortage areas	Up to 100 percent
Full-time employee of a public or nonprofit child- or family-services agency providing services to high-risk children and their families from low-income communities	Up to 100 percent
Full-time nurse or medical technician	Up to 100 percent
Full-time law enforcement or corrections officer	Up to 100 percent
Full-time staff member in the education component of a Head Start Program	Up to 100 percent
VISTA or Peace Corps volunteer	Up to 70 percent
Service in the U.S. Armed Forces	Up to 100 percent in areas of hostilities or imminent danger

Note: As of Oct. 7, 1998, all Perkins Loan borrowers are eligible for all cancellation benefits regardless of when the loan was made or the terms of the borrower's promissory note. However, this benefit is not retroactive to services performed before Oct. 7, 1998.

Table 14.

Conditions for Stafford and PLUS loan cancellation/discharge and amount forgiven

Cancellation Conditions	Amount Forgiven	Notes
Borrower's total and permanent disability or death.+	100 percent	For a PLUS Loan, circumstances include the death, but not disability, of the student for whom the parents borrowed.
Full-time teacher for five consecutive years in a designated elementary or secondary school or educational service agency serving students from low-income families. Must meet additional eligibility requirements. Teaching at an educational service agency may count toward the required five consecutive years only if the consecutive five-year period includes teaching service at an educational service agency performed after the 2007–08 academic year. PLUS Loans are not eligible.	Up to $5,000 (up to $17,500 for teachers in certain specialties) of the total loan amount outstanding after completion of the fifth year of teaching. Under the Direct Consolidation Loan programs, only the portion of the consolidation loan used to repay eligible Direct Loans qualifies for loan forgiveness.	For Direct and FFEL Stafford Loan borrowers with no outstanding balance on a Direct or FFEL Loan on Oct. 1, 1998, or on the date they received a loan on, or after that date. At least one of the five consecutive years of teaching in an elementary/secondary school must occur after the 1997–98 academic year. Teaching at an educational service agency may count toward the required five consecutive years only if the consecutive five-year period includes teaching service at an educational service agency performed after the 2007–08 academic year. To find out whether your school is considered a low-income school, go to: www.studentaid.ed.gov/tc. Or call 1-800-4-FED-AD (1-800-433-3243).
Bankruptcy (in rare cases)	100 percent	Cancellation is possible only if the bankruptcy court rules that repayment would cause undue hardship.
Closed school (before student could complete program of study) or false loan certification.	100 percent	This is for loans received on or after Jan. 1, 1986.
False loan certification includes identity theft.	100 percent	This is effective July 1, 2006.
School does not make required return of loan funds to the lender.	Up to the amount that the school was required to return.	This is for loans received on or after Jan. 1, 1986.
Loan forgiveness for public service employees.	100 percent of the remaining outstanding balance on an eligible Direct Loan. FFEL borrowers may qualify by consolidating into the Direct Loan Program.	For a borrower not in default and who makes 120 monthly payments, under certain repayment plans, on the loan while the borrower is employed full-time in a public service job after Oct. 1, 2007.

+ Total and permanent disability is defined as the inability to work and earn money because of an illness or injury that is expected to continue indefinitely or result in death. Your loan may be discharged if you are determined to be totally and permanently disabled based on a physician's certification, and if you meet certain other requirements during a three-year conditional discharge period.

Further information on teaching service cancellation options can be found at **www.studentaid.ed.gov/tc.**

A loan, whether in default or not, cannot be discharged in bankruptcy in most cases.

How do I find out if I can get a loan discharge or cancellation?

After reviewing the conditions, if you think you qualify, contact your loan servicer. For Perkins Loans check with the school that made you the loan or with the school's loan servicing agent. For other loans contact the loan servicer.

Repay

GLOSSARY

Accrue When interest on your loan adds to the amount you owe. The phrase "interest accruing on your loan" means that the amount of interest due on your loan is accumulating.

Aggregate loan limit The maximum total outstanding loan debt you can have when you graduate.

Borrower An individual who signed and agreed to the terms in the promissory note and is responsible for repaying a loan.

Capitalization Adding unpaid interest to the loan amount borrowed. Capitalization increases the unpaid principal balance of your loan and interest is charged on the increased principal amount. This occurs at the end of a deferment, forbearance, or grace period on unsubsidized loans, and at the end of a forbearance period on any type of loan, subsidized or unsubsidized. This increases the total amount you will repay over the life of your loan. To save money, pay interest before it's capitalized.

Consolidation The process of combining one or more eligible federal education loans into a single new loan.

Cost of Attendance (COA) The total amount it will cost you to go to school—usually expressed as a yearly figure. It's determined using rules established by law. The COA includes tuition and fees; on campus room and board (or a housing and food allowance for off-campus students); and allowances for books, supplies, transportation, loan fees, and, if applicable, dependent care. It also includes miscellaneous and personal expenses, including an allowance for the rental or purchase of a personal computer. Costs related to a disability also are covered. The COA includes reasonable costs for eligible study-abroad programs as well. For students attending less than half-time, the COA includes tuition and fees and an allowance for books, supplies, transportation, and dependent care expenses; and also can include room and board for up to three semesters, or the equivalent, at the institution—but no more than two of those semesters, or the equivalent, may be consecutive. Talk to the financial aid administrator at the school you're planning to attend if you have any unusual expenses that might affect your cost of attendance.

Credit A summary of a person's financial strength, including his or her history of paying bills, routinely used to assess a person's ability to repay future loans. Students often are turned down for private loans because they have not established a credit history and have no income with which to repay debts. People who pay their bills after the due date, have defaulted on debts, or declared bankruptcy are usually judged to have poor credit. Several private companies gather consumers' financial information to create reports used by businesses and lenders to determine how much to lend and how much interest to charge each consumer. Federal law requires credit rating agencies to provide consumers with one free report regarding their credit each year.

Credit Bureau Organization that tracks and reports the manner in which borrowers repay their loans (not only student loans).

Data Release Number Your DRN is a four-digit number assigned to your application by Federal Student Aid. It will appear close to the top right-hand corner on the first page of your paper or electronic *Student Aid Report* (SAR). If you file electronically, you also will find your DRN below the Confirmation Number on your submission confirmation page.

You will need the DRN if you contact the Federal Student Aid Information Center to make corrections to your mailing address or to the schools you listed on your FAFSA. The DRN also allows you to release your FAFSA data to schools you did not list on your original FAFSA.

Default Failure to repay a loan according to the terms of the promissory note. There can be serious legal consequences for student-loan defaulters.

Deferment A postponement of payment on a loan that is allowed under certain conditions and during which interest does not accrue for subsidized loans.

Delinquent Your loan payments are not received by the due dates. If your accounts have become delinquent and you are unable to make payments consider deferment, forbearance, or switching repayment plans. Accounts remain delinquent until borrowers bring their accounts current with payments, deferment, or forbearance.

Dependent Student Student who does not meet any of the criteria for an independent student. An independent student is defined as being any of the following: at least 24 years old, married, a graduate or professional student, a veteran, a member of the armed forces, an orphan, a ward of the court, someone with legal dependents other than a spouse, an emancipated minor, or is homeless or at risk of being homeless. If you answer "No" to any of these questions, you are a dependent student. Please see the fact sheet "Am I Dependent or Independent?" at **www.studentaid.ed.gov/pubs** for more detailed information.

Direct Consolidation Loan Federal program that allows you to combine one or more federal student loans into one new Direct Consolidation Loan. Only one monthly payment is made to the U.S. Department of Education. In certain circumstances, students who have loans under the Federal Family Education Loan Program (FFEL) may consolidate them into Direct Loans.

Direct PLUS Loan Unsubsidized loans available to parents of dependent students, and to students enrolled in graduate or professional programs. These loans are available regardless of financial need and the amount of eligibility depends on the total cost of education.

Direct Subsidized Loan Also known as the Federal Direct Subsidized Stafford Loan. A loan from the U.S. Department of Education made on the basis of the student's financial need and other specific eligibility requirements. The federal government does not charge interest on these loans while borrowers are enrolled at least half-time, during a six-month grace period, or during authorized periods of deferment.

Direct Unsubsidized Loan Also known as the Federal Direct Unsubsidized Stafford Loan. A federally financed student loan made to students meeting specific eligibility requirements. Interest is charged throughout the life of the loan. The borrower may choose to pay the interest charged on the loan during in-school, grace, deferment, and forbearance periods, or allow the interest to be capitalized (added to the loan principal).

Disbursement Payment of loan proceeds to the borrower by the school. During consolidation, this term refers to sending payoffs to the loan holders of the underlying loans being consolidated.

Due Date (Payment Due Date) Date during the month when payment of your current due amount must be received. If you have any past due amounts or fees or outstanding charges, these are due immediately.

Monthly payments must be received by the payment due date. Therefore, if you do not have your payments debited electronically from a bank account, you may want to mail your payments well in advance to ensure they arrive and are applied to your account(s) by the due date(s).

Entrance Counseling An information session which takes place before the loan is disbursed and is required for first-time borrowers. The session explains your responsibilities and rights as a student borrower.

Exit Counseling Borrower receives a notice about exit counseling when borrower graduates or attends school less than half-time. At this session, the borrower will be given information on your loans and when repayment begins.

Expected Family Contribution (EFC) An index used to determine your eligibility for federal student aid during one school year. You receive an EFC based on the processing results of your FAFSA. Your EFC is reported to you on your *Student Aid Report* (SAR).

FAFSA see *Free Application for Federal Student Aid*

FAFSA4caster An online tool designed to help students and families financially plan for college, you can get an early estimate of your federal student aid eligibility by using *FAFSA4caster*.

Federal Family Education Loan Program^{SM} (FFEL Program) A federal program that provided loans to eligible student and parent borrowers. The program consisted of Federal Subsidized and Unsubsidized Stafford Loans, Federal PLUS Loans, and Federal Subsidized and Unsubsidized Consolidation Loans. Funds were provided by private lenders, such as banks, credit unions, and other private financial institutions. The loans were backed by the federal government.

Note: As of July 1, 2010, no new loans were made under the FFEL Program.

Financial Aid Administrator (FAA) An individual who works at a college or career school and is responsible for preparing and communicating information on student loans, grants or scholarships, and employment programs. The FAA and staff help students apply for and receive student aid. The FAA is also capable of analyzing student needs and making professional judgment changes when necessary.

Forbearance A period during which your monthly loan payments are temporarily suspended or reduced. You may qualify for forbearance if you are unable to make loan payments due to certain types of financial hardships.

Free Application for Federal Student Aid (FAFSA) The FAFSA or *FAFSA on the Web*, the online version, is the FREE application used to apply for federal student aid.

Grace Period A six-month period that begins on the day after you, the Stafford Loan Program borrower, cease to be enrolled as at least a half-time student at an eligible institution and ends on the day before the repayment period begins.

Half-time Student

(1) An enrolled student who is carrying a half-time academic workload, as determined by the institution, that amounts to at least half of the workload of the applicable minimum requirement outlined in the definition of a full-time student.

(2) A student enrolled solely in a program of study by correspondence who is carrying a workload of at least 12 hours of work per week, or is earning at least six credit hours per semester, trimester, or quarter. However, regardless of the work, no student enrolled solely in correspondence study is considered more than a half-time student.

These minimum requirements apply to undergraduate students.

Independent Student Must meet any of the following criteria: at least 24 years old, married, a graduate or professional student, a veteran, a member of the armed forces, an orphan, a ward of the court, someone with legal dependents other than a spouse, an emancipated minor, or is homeless or at risk of homelessness. Please see the fact sheet "Am I Dependent or Independent?" at **www.studentaid.ed.gov/pubs** for more detailed information.

Interest A loan expense charged by the lender and paid by the borrower for the use of borrowed money. The expense is calculated as a percentage of the unpaid principal amount (loan amount), which includes the original amount borrowed and any capitalized interest (unpaid interest added to the principal loan amount). Accrued interest is interest that accumulates on the unpaid principal balance of the loan.

Interest Rate The current rate at which interest is calculated on your loan(s).

Lender The organization that made the loan initially. The lender could be the borrower's school (for Federal Perkins Loans); a bank, credit union, or other lending institution; or the U.S. Department of Education.

Loan Money borrowed from a lending institution or the U.S. Department of Education that must be repaid.

Loan Fee A fee payable by the borrower that is deducted proportionately from each loan disbursement.

Loan Servicer An organization that administers and collects education loans payments on behalf of the lender.

National Student Loan Data System (NSLDS) A centralized database that stores information on all Department loans and grants. NSLDS also contains borrowers' school enrollment information. Borrowers can access this information online using their Department of Education PIN at **www.nslds.ed.gov**.

Parent Borrower Parents that have at least one PLUS Loan to finance their dependent child's education.

Partial Financial Hardship A circumstance in which:

for an unmarried borrower or a married borrower who files an individual federal tax return, the annual amount due on all of the borrower's eligible loans—as calculated under a standard repayment plan based on a 10-year repayment period, using the greater of either the amount due at the time the borrower initially entered repayment or at the time the borrower elects the income-based repayment plan—exceeds a certain percentage of the difference between the borrower's adjusted gross income and the poverty guideline for the borrower's family size; or

for a married borrower who files a joint federal tax return with his or her spouse, the annual amount due on all of the borrower's eligible loans and, if applicable, the spouse's eligible loans—as calculated under a standard repayment plan based on a 10-year repayment period, using the greater of either the amount due at the time the loans initially entered repayment or at the time the borrower or spouse elects the income-based repayment plan—exceeds a certain percentage of the difference between the borrower's and spouse's adjusted gross income, and the poverty guideline for the borrower's family size.

Eligible loan means any outstanding loan made to a borrower under the FFEL or Direct Loan programs except for a defaulted loan, an FFEL or Direct PLUS Loan made to a parent borrower, or an FFEL or Direct Consolidation Loan that repaid an FFEL or Direct PLUS Loan made to a parent borrower.

Past Due The amount that you were scheduled to pay in previous month(s) but did not. The past due amount is also called the delinquent amount. Your account is considered "delinquent" if you have missed any monthly payments. Past Due amounts are due immediately.

Payment Due Date The date during the month when payment of your current due amount must be received. If you have any past due amounts or fees and outstanding charges, these are due immediately. Monthly payments must be received by the payment due date. Therefore, if you do not have your payments debited electronically from a bank account, you may want to mail your payments well in advance to ensure they arrive and are applied to your account(s) by the due date.

Perkins Loans Formerly known as National Defense Student Loan, or National Direct Student Loan. Federal Perkins Loans are low-interest (5%) loans for both undergraduate and graduate students with exceptional financial need. Your school is the lender. The loans are made with government funds with a share contributed by the school. You must repay these loans to your school.

PIN (Federal Student Aid PIN) Serves as your identifier to allow access to personal information in various U.S. Department of Education systems.

Your PIN also acts as your digital signature with some online forms. Use your PIN to electronically sign your online FAFSA, consolidation loan application and promissory note and deferment or forbearance forms.

If you do not already have a PIN, you can request one online at **www.pin.ed.gov**. The PIN you receive will be your universal U.S. Department of Education PIN.

Prepayment The amount in excess of the amount due on a loan. If borrowers have more than one federal student loan, they must specify which loan they are prepaying. Like all other federal student loan payments, a prepayment will first be applied to any outstanding fees and charges, next to outstanding interest, and then to the principal balance of the loan(s). There is never a penalty for prepaying principal or interest on federal student loans.

Promissory Note A binding legal document you sign when you get a student loan. It contains the loan terms and conditions under which you're borrowing and the terms under which you agree to pay back the loan. It will include deferment and cancellation provisions available to the borrower. It's very important to read and save this document because you'll need to refer to it later when you begin repaying your loan or at other times when you need information about provisions of the loan, such as deferments or forbearances.

Refund The total amount of funds returned to the loan program as unused for the student's education expenses.

Rehabilitation The process of bringing a loan out of default and removing the default notation on a borrower's credit report. To rehabilitate a Direct or an FFEL Loan, you must make at least nine full payments of an agreed amount within 20 days of their monthly due dates over a 10-month period to the U.S. Department of Education. To rehabilitate a Perkins Loan, you must make nine, on-time, monthly payments of an agreed amount to the Department. Rehabilitation terms and conditions vary for other loan types and can be obtained from the loan servicer.

Repayment Incentive A benefit that the U.S. Department of Education offers borrowers to encourage them to repay their loans on time. Under a repayment incentive program, the interest rate charged on borrowers' loans might be reduced. Some repayment incentive programs require borrowers to make a certain number of payments on time to keep the benefits of the repayment incentive.

Repayment Plan An agreed schedule between a borrower and a lender on repayment of a loan. Changing repayment plans is a good way to manage your loan debt when your financial circumstances change to a less favorable status. For example, you can usually lower your monthly payment by changing to another repayment plan that has a longer term in which to repay the loan. There are no penalties for changing repayment plans.

Repayment Schedule A statement provided by the loan servicer to the borrower that lists the amount borrowed, the amount of monthly payments, and the date payments are due.

Repayment Term The number of months it will take to repay your federal student loans under a specific repayment plan.

Servicer An entity designated to track and collect a loan on behalf of a loan holder.

Simple Daily Interest The method used to calculate interest on your student loans. To learn more about how interest is calculated, see page 19.

Student Aid Report (SAR) This report has your FAFSA results and details all the information you provided on your FAFSA. If there are no corrections or additional information you must provide, the SAR will contain your EFC, which is the number that's used to determine your eligibility for federal student aid. Whether you applied online or by paper, we will automatically send your data electronically to the schools you listed on your FAFSA.

Total Amount Repaid The total amount you would be expected to pay over the life of the loan, including principal and interest.

Variable Interest The rate of interest charged on a loan that changes annually and fluctuates with a stated index.

William D. Ford Federal Direct Loan Program (Direct Loan Program) The federal program that provides loans to eligible student and parent borrowers. Funds are provided directly by the federal government to eligible borrowers through participating schools. The loan program includes Direct Subsidized Loans, Direct Unsubsidized Loans, Direct PLUS Loans, and Direct Consolidation Loans.

Things to Remember

- Student loans are an investment in your future.
- Make a budget and stick with it. Be careful with credit card spending.
- Borrow only what you need.
- If you don't understand something, call your lender or your financial aid office.
- Keep all student loan documents in a file.
- Open all your mail and read everything pertaining to your student loans.
- Keep in contact with your servicer.
- Make all regularly scheduled payments.
- Ask your lender for help if you start to have difficulty making payments. There are alternative options available.
- Borrowing is an investment in your future.

Don't Default

You've made a commitment to yourself and your future. Be a responsible borrower, because loan default has serious consequences:

- Your entire loan balance (principal and interest) will be due in full immediately.
- Your college records may be placed on hold.
- You'll lose your student loan deferment options.
- You won't be eligible for additional federal student aid.
- Your account may be turned over to a collection agency and you'll have to pay additional charges, late fees, and collection costs, all of which become part of your debt.
- Your credit rating will be damaged for several years because defaulted loans are reported to national credit bureaus.
- You'll have difficulty qualifying for credit cards, a car loan, a mortgage, or renting an apartment (credit checks are required even to rent an apartment).
- Your federal and state income tax refunds can be withheld and applied to student loan debt. This is called a tax offset.
- You may have a portion of your wages garnished (withheld).
- You may not be able to obtain a professional license or get hired by any employer that performs credit checks on its prospective employees.

Any Questions?

If you ever have any questions on federal student aid, visit the websites listed on the inside of the front cover. If you still have questions and need to talk to someone:

- call us at **1-800-4-FED-AID (1-800-433-3243)**,
- talk to your high school counselor, or
- contact the financial aid office at the school you plan on attending.